Wow!
Look What
Your Body
Can Do!

KINGFISHER
LONDON & NEW YORK

Copyright © Macmillan Publishers International Ltd 2013, 2018
Published in the United States by Kingfisher,
175 Fifth Ave., New York, NY 10010
Kingfisher is an imprint of Macmillan Children's Books, London

Distributed in the U.S. and Canada by Macmillan,
175 Fifth Ave., New York, NY 10010
Library of Congress Cataloging-in-Publication data has been applied for.

Author: Jacqueline McCann and Emma Dods
Design and styling: Liz Adcock
Cover design: Liz Adcock
Illustrations: Marc Aspinall & Ste Johnson

ISBN: 978-0-7534-7483-9 (HB)
ISBN: 978-0-7534-7473-0 (PB)

Illustrations in this book previously appeared in *Wow! Human Body*,
published by Kingfisher in 2013.

Kingfisher books are available for special promotions and premiums.
For details contact: Special Markets Department, Macmillan,
175 Fifth Ave., New York, NY 10010.

For more information, please visit
www.kingfisherbooks.com

Printed in China
9 8 7 6 5 4 3 2 1
1TR/0418/WKT/UG/140WFO

Wow!
Look What
Your Body
Can Do!

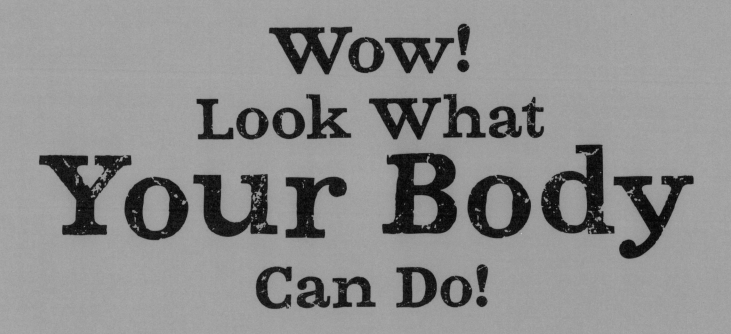

KINGFISHER
KNOW | WONDER

What are we?

Human beings come in all shapes and sizes, but mostly we're all the same.

On the outside, people look different to one another. We may have different colored skin, eyes, and hair . . .

. . . but we all have a body, a head, legs, and arms. And on the inside, we have a brain, a heart, and lots of other organs that help our body work.

We are women.

I am a man.

we're kids!

My dark skin **protects** me from the sun!

Some people have dark skin. Some people have light skin. Most people have skin that is a shade of brown.

We're cells. We're tiny...

...but very important!

Wow!

Your body is mostly made of water. You also have 37,000,000,000,000 cells in your body! That's 37 trillion!

I'm a nerve cell.

Cells are the building blocks of all living things. Everything that goes on in your body happens because of your cells. You have roughly 200 different kinds of cell.

I'm a red blood cell.

Your cells work together all the time to build organs, such as your brain and your heart. They protect your body, too, and help to fight off disease and sickness.

We're super-strong muscle cells!

I'm a white blood cell.

Growing up

We all start life as a lump of cells. Gradually, we grow from baby to child and then to grown-up!

You start life as tiny cells!

gurgle

Children grow quickly and learn to become more independent. They are often very lively. Are you?

When you're a baby, you have a big head and short legs, but you grow very fast! A baby needs lots of love!

You grow fastest in spring and summer!

Getting bigger

When you are a newborn baby, you need an adult to take care of you. As you grow, you become more independent and need adults less and less.

When you're a teenager, your body starts to change—a lot!

By the time you are 18 years old, you are an adult and your body has done most of its growing!

When you're 45, you start to slow down. You don't have as much energy as you did before. Oh dear!

Not so fast, kiddo!

Go gray

You're body might stop growing when you're an adult . . . but your nose and ears keep getting bigger! Your bones aren't as strong as they were, and your hair will probably turn gray.

What big ears you've got, Dear!

Big bones, little bones

What holds you up? Your bones, of course! If you didn't have them, you'd be like wobbly jello.

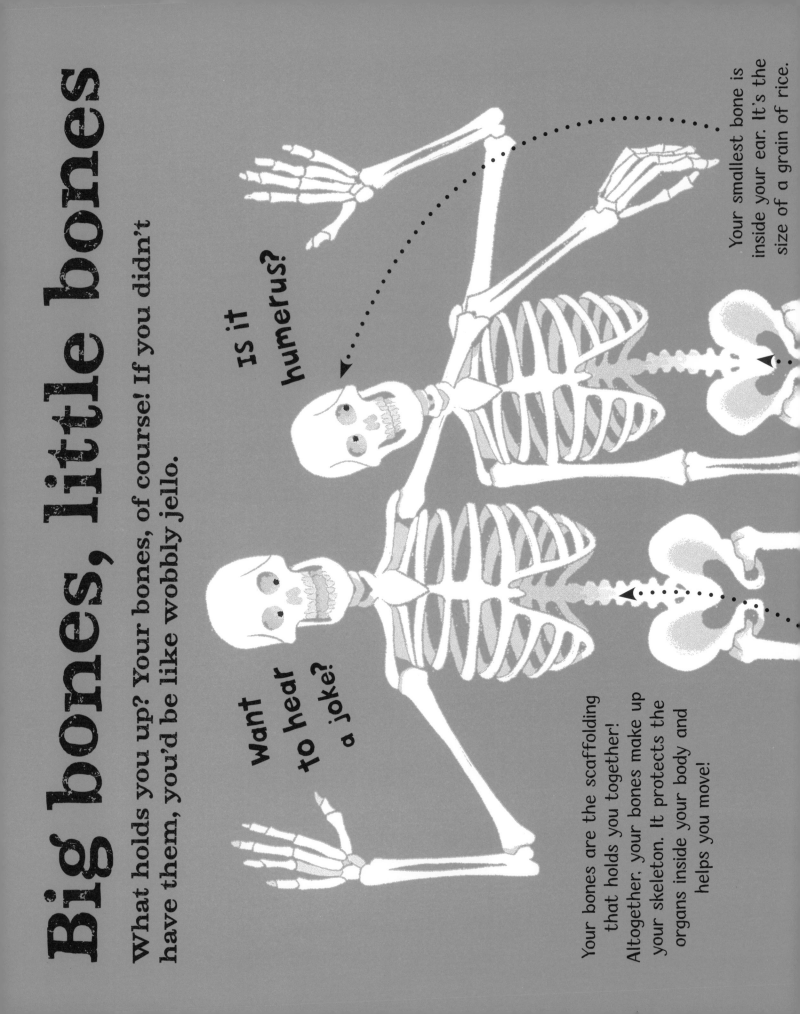

is it humerus?

want to hear a joke?

Your bones are the scaffolding that holds you together! Altogether, your bones make up your skeleton. It protects the organs inside your body and helps you move!

Your smallest bone is inside your ear. It's the size of a grain of rice.

Your spine is a chain of bones running down your back. Your spine and leg bones help you to stand and walk.

At the bottom of your spine (in your butt) are four tiny bones joined together, like a mini tail!

i've got a tail, too!

The strongest and longest bone in your body is in your leg—it's called the femur.

You have 52 bones in your two feet.

When you're a baby, you have 300 to 350 bones. As you grow, small bones in your body stick, or fuse, together. By the time you're a grown-up you'll have 206 bones.

Wow!

Your skull is like a hard hat protecting your brain. It's made of 22 bones that stick together as you grow. Your teeth are part of your skeleton, too!

9

Muscle power

More than half your body is made of muscles. Their main job is to get your body moving!

Muscles support your skeleton and keep your shape. They help you walk, jump, run, and win races!

MOVE OVER, we're coming through!

I'm the fastest. I've got four legs!

When you start to run, your brain sends a message to your muscles and bones to get going! Your muscles work in pairs with your bones, stretching and relaxing.

Wow!

There are more than 650 named muscles in the human body. Did you know that you use 300 just to stand?

Did you know your muscles have memory! The more you practice something, the better your muscles become at remembering, which is important when you learn a new sport.

FINISH

oh my gluteus!

Ouch!

Your muscles protect your bones if you fall. Your largest muscle is in your butt! It's called the gluteus (say *gloot-y-us*) maximus.

You use 17 muscles when you smile!

Heart and blood

Blood is the red liquid that fuels your body. Your heart does the hard work pumping it around your body.

Pump it up

Your heart is like two super-strong muscles working together like pumps. It squeezes blood around your body, then relaxes before squeezing again.

Your blood is super stuff! It has tiny cells that carry everything your body needs to help you breathe, keep you warm, fight off diseases, think, and grow!

Blood vessels and arteries are like roads that carry blood around your body.

Red blood cells carry oxygen.

Wow!

Your heart works very hard—it beats about 90 times a minute. It will beat about three billion times in your lifetime!

White blood cells fight disease!

Big heart

Your heart grows as you grow. You can't see your heart, but it sits behind your ribs, slightly on the left-hand side.

How can you take care of your heart? Do lots of exercise every day, eat all your fruit and vegetables, and drink lots of water!

Let's hop, skip, and jump...

Your heart, blood and arteries work together to carry vitamins from food around your body and keep you in good working order. They also carry away any chemicals your body doesn't need.

Control center

Your brain is smarter and more powerful than the world's most powerful computer!

Your brain collects messages from your body and the world around you. It stores all the information it receives for you to use when you need to!

I'm brainy...

This part is good at reading and knowing left from right.

The front part of your brain works out language and math.

The back of your brain recognizes color.

This part controls movement.

skip, don't trip!

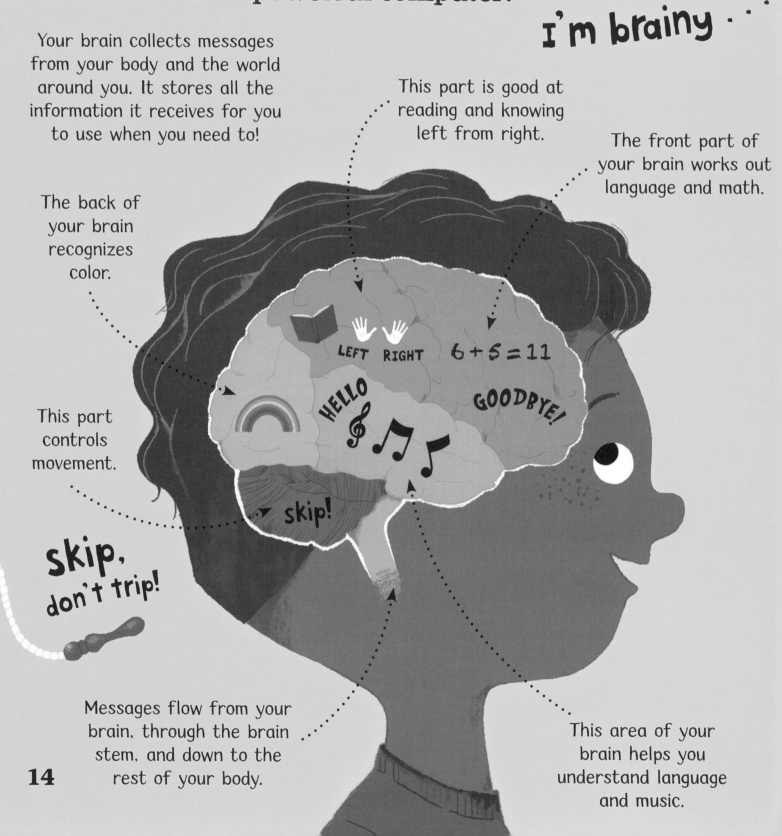

LEFT RIGHT 6 + 5 = 11

HELLO

GOODBYE!

skip!

Messages flow from your brain, through the brain stem, and down to the rest of your body.

14

This area of your brain helps you understand language and music.

. . . but an elephant's brain is **bigger!**

Wow!

An elephant has the biggest brain of any animal on land. Its brain is four times bigger than an adult human's.

Chimpanzees are smart, too. They use tools to do jobs (like us), and they are almost unbeatable at some computer games!

Any more bananas?

Rats and mice are quick learners and they're good at puzzles!

I'm smart, too.

Skin and hair

Skin wraps around your skeleton and muscles, keeping it all together. What else does it do?

Your skin is like a waterproof coat; it keeps the rain and the germs out. It stops all your blood and gooey parts from leaking out, too!

Wow!

The surface of your skin is constantly rubbing off in tiny flakes as new skin is made underneath. The dust in your house is mostly made of those tiny flakes!

Hi, I'm a mighty dust mite!

Yummy!

Teeny tiny creatures called dust mites live in your house, munching on dead flakes of your skin—they're everywhere, but they're too small to see.

16

You have hair ALL over your body. The only place you don't have it is the palms of your hands, the soles of your feet, and your lips!

The roots of your hair, called follicles, grow from your skin, too. You even have hairs up your nose. They trap dust and germs so you don't breathe dirt in.

It's true
Straight hair grows from round follicles. Curly hair grows from oval follicles.

What color is your hair?

I have hair on my top lip. It's called a mustache.

Red hair is the rarest hair color in the world.

Blond-haired people have more hairs on their head than other people.

Everyone loses 50-150 hairs a day. Mine didn't grow back!

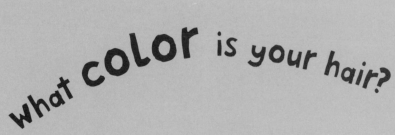

Eyes and ears

You have five main senses that allow you to connect to the world: smell, touch, taste, sight, and hearing.

who's a pretty Polly?

Your eyes are on the front of your face, looking forward. This means you can see in front of you and a little to the sides, but you can't see behind you.

Light enters your pupil—the black dot in the middle of your eye—but it's your brain that tells you what you are seeing!

I spy

Your eyes are so powerful that they can take in more information than the world's largest telescope.

I hear you, Captain!

Ear, ear

Some animals, such as rabbits, swivel their ears when they want to hear a sound, but your ears are shaped to catch sounds and channel them into your ear.

Animals and birds are often better at seeing and hearing than you are.

squawk!

A macaw is a kind of parrot. It has eyes on either side of its head, which means it can see all around, even behind!

Wow!

Ears don't just help you to hear, they help you to balance, too. They tell your body that you're lying down at night, or standing up in the day!

Like all parrots, macaws are very good listeners. They can hear high-pitched sounds that people can't hear.

Smell, taste, touch

Imagine if you couldn't smell your favorite dinner, or taste a crunchy apple? What if you couldn't touch?

How do you know if something smells stinky, sweet, or sour? Smart little cells at the back of your nose send a message to your brain to let you know!

cake feels squidgy . . .

Sniff . . .

If you didn't have a sense of touch, you wouldn't be able to tell if something is hot, cold, itchy, painful, or very heavy!

As you grow older, you gradually lose your sense of smell and taste.

A baby learns how things feel by putting them into its mouth!

Your sense of smell is connected to your memory, too. Freshly cut grass might make you think of a summer picnic. Or maybe smelly socks make you think of your big brother!

smells yummy . . . and tastes delicious!

Wow!

Your nose recognizes more than 10,000 different smells! And it's your sense of smell that actually tells you most about what you are tasting!

The first sense a baby uses when it's born is smell!

Your tongue is the most sensitive part of your body. It has nearly 5,000 taste buds to help you taste different flavors.

Grapes on the loose . . .

Down it goes

What happens to your lunch after you've smelled, tasted, and eaten it? Let's see!

When food is in your mouth, your body starts to break it up into little pieces. First your teeth go to work . . .

Open wide. Lunch on its way!

1
Sharp teeth do the cutting.

2
Molar teeth at the back do the crushing.

3
A juice called saliva mixes with your food.

4
Your tongue helps push food to the back of your mouth.

5
The jiggly uvula stops food going the wrong way!

The journey's just beginning for lunch— it still has a long way to travel before it goes all the way down to . . . the bottom—or the butt!

crrrrunch!

1
The juicy apple is squeezed down a long tube, called the gullet.

3
Food travels into your intestines where more juices break it up. All the good stuff is sent around your body.

2
When the apple reaches your stomach, strong juices kill all the germs.

4
Anything your body doesn't want is passed out here as poop and urine, or . . .

paaarrp!

Windy tummy

Sometimes gas escapes from your body, either through a burp or a fart! Has this ever happened to you?

It takes more than a day for food to go in one end and out the other. Your body pushes out what it doesn't need as poop and urine.

When you eat and drink, you breathe in air which is made of gases. Bacteria in your intestines make gas too. Eventually all those gases need to come out as . . .

You guessed it!

Farting and burping is . . .

paaarrp!

. . . noisy but normal!

You will spend about three years of your life on the toilet. Yeeeew!

Farty food!

Beans, cabbage, artichokes, peas, apples, and sprouts all make you fart more. But they are very good for you!

Scientists have spent a long time studying what happens when astronauts fart in space! The farts don't go anywhere— they just hover!

Astronaut suits are fitted with special filters that get rid of poisonous gases!

In **Space,** no one can hear you . . .

. . . **fart!**

Is it nighttime?

Night, night

Why is sleeping so important? Does your body do anything when it is fast asleep?

It takes most people 7 minutes to fall asleep.

Sleeping helps you to remember things and to learn, which is why you have to go to bed early on a school night! Children need between 10 and 12 hours sleep a night!

While you're sleeping, your body works very hard for you, growing muscles and bones, and making itself better.

Zzzzz!

Wow!
You will spend about a third of your life sleeping! So if you live to be 90 years old, that's 30 years of snoozing!

What happens if you don't get enough sleep? Your body doesn't work so well, your reactions are slower and it's more difficult to concentrate. You'll probably be a little grumpy, too!

Sweet dreams!

Why dream?

No one knows for sure why we dream. Scientists think it might be a good way to sort our memories, or to clear your brain after you've had a hard day's work.

Some people do unbelievable things when they're asleep! They go for a walk (that's sleepwalking) or play the piano. Sleepwalkers can even cook or draw amazing pictures.

Shhhhh! More amazing body facts this way . . .

27

Amazing body

Your body does lots of amazing things, without you telling it to—these are called reflexes.

Tee-hee-hee! Giggle! Giggle!

You may think you are in control of your body, but it's your reflexes that make you . . .

. . . blink if something touches your eye.

Ticklish?

It is impossible to tickle yourself because your brain knows what is coming and ignores the "tickle." It only works if someone else does it for you!

. . . yawn when you feel sleepy.

. . . hiccup without knowing why.

. . . cough and sneeze. Achoo!

tickle tickle!

. . . shiver when you're cold . . . and sometimes when you're scared!

Keep still!

I can't!

Standing on one leg isn't easy! But even to stand on two legs, you have to keep shifting your weight, or you'll fall!

If you take 8,000 to 10,000 steps a day, then in your lifetime, you will have walked the same distance as four times around the world!

Time to get moving! Walk this way . . .

where are we going?

Wow!

Have you you ever noticed the swirly patterns on your fingertips? Those patterns are called fingerprints. No one else has the same patterns as you!

It's true

It isn't only your fingerprints that are unique to you—no one has the same toe prints either! Your lips, earlobes, tongue print, and teeth are all unique to you, too!

Ancient body facts

Thousands of years ago, the ancient Egyptians and Romans had some funny ideas about bodies!

The ancient Egyptians were a smart bunch—they built the pyramids after all! But strange as it seems to us, when cats died, their owners shaved off their eyebrows!

My cat died. NOW I have to shave my eyebrows!

Ancient Egyptian kings, called pharaohs, had people who worked for them as official butt wipers!

Squeak

Nearly 3,000 years ago, in ancient Egypt, if you had bad breath, the dentist put a hot, dead mouse in your mouth to cure you. Eeeek!

Ancient Romans used pigeon droppings to lighten their hair!

SPLAT!

Wow!

Ancient Romans thought that broken ribs could be healed by applying a mixture of goat's poop and wine to the chest.

The Romans were the first people to build real hospitals. And a famous Roman doctor called Galen discovered that blood flows through arteries.

The slime from garden snails was used to treat burns and nosebleeds in ancient Rome!

Slide this way for stinky stuff!

Stinky stuff

Have you noticed that your body makes a lot of gunk? From sweaty feet, to poop, snot, and earwax!

In the Middle Ages (that's about 650 years ago) people used snail slime to treat a sore throat!

Your feet are the sweatiest part of your body. But sweat keeps the skin on your feet soft and flexible so you can walk, run, and dance!

Earwax is sticky stuff that keeps your ears clean and keeps the bugs away!

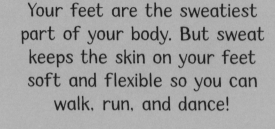

Earwax can be yellow, gray, orange, or green!

Achoo!

Wow!

Your body makes more than two pints (1 liter) of snotty mucus every day. That's about the size of a carton of juice! Mucus does a great job of keeping your airways clear and protecting you from bugs!

Your sneeze travels at nearly 100 miles (160 km) per hour and carries about 100,000 germs. Keep the tissues handy!